"I lay my wing
As a bridge to you
So that you can join us
Singing."

Hafiz
"A Crystal Rim"

Footprints Wings Phantasms

Other Books by This Author

Shadow Dancing: $elling $urvival in China. Ka`a`awa, HI: Pacific Raven Press. 2017.

Zimbabwe Spin: Politics and Poetics. Ka`a`awa, HI: Pacific Raven Press, 2015.

Love's Seasons: Generations Genetics Myths. Ka`a`awa, HI: Pacific Raven Press, 2014.

Timmy Turtle Teaches. Children's book. Ka`a`awa, HI: Pacific Raven Press, 2012.

Frank Marshall Davis: The Fire and the Phoenix (A Critical Biography). Ka`a`awa, HI: Pacific Raven Press, 2012.

Tourmalines: Beyond the Ebony Portal. Ka`a`awa, HI: Pacific Raven Press, 2010.

***Pacific Raven: Hawai`i Poems***. Ka`a`awa, HI: Pacific Raven Press, 2009. (Winner of 2010 American Book Award from the Before Columbus Foundation.)

New and Collected Poems. Berkeley, CA: Ishmael Reed Publishing, 2003.

Oral Histories of African Americans. Interviews by Kathryn Waddell Takara. Center for Oral History. Social Science Research Institute. Honolulu, HI: University of Hawai`i at Mānoa, 1990.

Footprints Wings Phantasms

Awake
   Experience
      Understand
            . . . Transform

Kathryn Waddell Takara, PhD

Edited by Mera Moore

Pacific Raven Press
Ka`a`awa, Hawai`i
http://pacificravenpress.co

© 2018 by Kathryn Waddell Takara, Pacific Raven Press, LLC

All rights reserved. This book may not be reproduced, in whole or in part, including illustrations, in any form (beyond that copying permitted by Sections 107 and 108 of the U.S. Copyright Law and except by reviewers for the public press), without written permission from the publisher.

Pacific Raven Press, LLC
Ka`a`awa, Hawai`i 96730

ISBN: 978-0-9860755-8-2
Ebook: 978-09993039-0-0

Cover Design and Concept:
Kathryn Waddell Takara and Jonathan Zane

Book Layout: Jonathan Zane, Eien Design
www.eiendesignstudio.com

Contributing Editor: Nancy Jones Karp

Executive Editor: Mera Moore

This work is licensed under Pacific Raven Press, LLC.

Library of Congress Cataloging-in-publication data
Footprints Wings Phantasms by Kathryn Waddell Takara, PhD
Catalogued as: Philosophy, Poetry, Psychology

Printed in the United States of America

Pacific Raven Press, LLC, is an independent publisher.
http://pacificravenpress.co/
pacificravenpress@yahoo.com

Dedication

To the Muse of Transformation

Table of Contents

Acknowledgements	xvii
Foreword by Peter Dong Feng, PhD	xxi
Preface	xxiii

SECTION I – AWAKE

Falling from the Sky	5
Tears of the Moon	6
Exposure	8
Seeing	9
Twisters of Fortune	10
No Comment	11
All Is Speculation	12
The Others	13
Libra	14
End of the River	15
Foreboding	16
Morning Meditation	17
Forces Unleashed	18

SECTION II – EXPERIENCE

Mirror Flower, Water Moon	23
Land and Sand	24
The Fall	25
Moon Magic	26
Pondering	27
Mama's Lap	28
Inquiries	30
Wings of Truth	31

The Mechanical Self	33
Meandering	34
Yearning	35
Unbirthed	37
Desert of Questions	38
Shout Hallelujah!	40
Orgasm of Honeybees	42
Seasoned Forgetfulness	44
Exit on Wings	45
Shifts out of Time	47

SECTION III – UNDERSTAND

Charming	53
All and Nothing	54
Wings of Transformation	55
Timeless Creation	57
On the Move	58
Orbs	59
Golden Philosophies	60
Sufi Story	61
Visible and Invisible	62
Strength in Words	64
Is There a Green Calling?	66
Astral Eyes	67
Glossary	69
About the Author	101

Acknowledgments

This collection is a poetic response to ***The Desert Swimmer*** by Peter Dong Feng, PhD, professor and poet at the University of Qingdao in China. Feng is a poet, scholar, and translator. He received a doctorate in English Literature from Nanjing University in 2011. Since then, he has been exploring consciousness in poetry from the perspectives of nature, philosophy, and psychoanalysis.

I humbly bow and am thankful to the ancestors, my husband Harvey Takara, daughters Karla Brundage and Natasha Harrington, granddaughter Asha Brundage-Moore, son-in-law Brad Harrington and the younger grandchildren Makalya, Zachary, and Mia, and many others with whom I have shared my years and memories turned into poems.

I extend my lasting gratitude to my **many** professional helpers, including Mera Moore, executive editor; Nancy Jones Karp, business director, marketing strategist, and contributing editor; Karla Brundage, assistant editor; Jonathan Zane, the ever-creative and patient graphic designer; and Olivia York, my skilled and supportive administrative and technological assistant.

I am very appreciative to scholars and publishers for their research support: Professor Allison Francis for her scholarly and editorial suggestions; the late Professor Paul Lyons for his years of support, both editorial and professional; Professor Cynthia Ning for her help and promotion with my Chinese projects; Lucy Lange Day for her camaraderie; Ishmael Reed for his friendship.

I am grateful to my **creative friends in Hawai`i, California, and beyond** who have encouraged my quest to produce and write by giving informal feedback on my poetry, sharing meals and music, supporting and contributing to my public events and private aspirations, and being there reliably when I needed to visit, talk, and laugh.

They include Daphne Barbee and Andre Wooten, Sandra Simms, Miles Jackson, Ayin Adams, Sharon Yarbrough, Tadia Rice, Iris Takata, Dr. Terry Shintani, Richard Hamasaki, Wing Tek Lum, and Imaikalani Kalahele.

I celebrate my **Ka`a`awa neighbors** for their encouragement and hugging playful support, including Scott Carter's accompanying guitar and percussion instruments for my poetry performances. Wendy Lagareta, Joan Koff, Andrea Anixt, Jeanne Scott, and Marya Foley helped this work to dance higher and sing louder.

I am deeply indebted to **friends in China.** You helped me during my eight visits to northeastern China, mainly Qingdao and Beijing. You invited, housed, fed, and cared deeply for me in your homes, communities, and universities. I owe all of you profound gratitude.

Deep thanks for the graciousness of friends in **Qingdao**. Who invited me to teach, and helped me to extend my reach of words, books, and philosophies, providing inspiration, insight, and cultural understanding. The late government minister Xue Rong Fang gave me invaluable introductions to jobs, government, and communities. With her generous compassion and *guanxi*, she opened doors. She is greatly missed. Philip Sue and family, and others, welcomed and guided me, and shared their culinary skills and celebrations, inviting me into their homes and communities. I'm especially thankful to faculty and administrators at the University of Qingdao: Professor Guo Cui, Professor Zhang Xiangming, Dean Bian Jianhua, and Professor Peter Dong Feng.

Also profound thanks to friends in **Beijing** for your hospitality, and for hosting me in your homes, universities, and communities. Retired Professor Gu Xiu Lin, scientist and organic farmer, communicated her knowledge of and passion for sustainable local agriculture. Zhang Yuan shared his artistic tie-dye cloth making, along with his skills as a tour guide and interpreter. Retired Professor Liu Zhengqing bestowed his talents as a calligrapher, tea master, and antiques expert. Thanks also go out to faculty and administration at the Beijing University of Foreign Studies: Professor and Vice Dean Fu Mei Rong; the excellent interpreter and Professor Li Jinzhao; and Professor of Chinese Law Russell K. L. Leu.

The **guides and teachers** too numerous to name individually deserve recognition for expanding the teachings of Gurdjieff and Ouspensky, aiding in my awakening on the path of mindfulness, development of conscience, and growth toward consciousness.

Much gratitude to the distinguished *taiji* and *qi* balance teacher, Master Wang Qing Chuang, who graciously shares his wisdom; and valued *taiji* teachers Geriann Almonte and Kathy Wang. For beneficial health maintenance, I thank Frasier Black.

I am honored to be a Knighted Dame of the nearly 1,000-year tradition of the Orthodox Order of St. John of Jerusalem (Russian Grand Priory). Many thanks to Countess Tatiana Bobrinskoy, Prior Terry Shintani, and other Knights and Dames, for introducing me to centuries-old rituals and this praiseworthy association.

Finally, I must express appreciation for my affiliation with various groups and associations that have offered me opportunities for new friendships and a platform to share my work. Groups that have challenged me to intellectual discussions are Pen Women (NLAPW); my book club, Bookies, which provide monthly reading assignments and discussions, plus food and wine; the Honolulu Chapter of The Links, Inc., sisters in public service; the Center for Chinese Studies at the University of Hawai`i at Mānoa, especially Cynthia Ning, Wu Qing, and Daniel Tschudi; the East Honolulu Rotary whose focus on service, networking, and commitment persuaded me to reach out internationally; Qingdao University; and Beijing University of Foreign Studies.

Foreword

By Peter Dong Feng, PhD

Kathryn Takara's incantations in her new book have taken a salubrious linguistic as well as speculative turn, turning invisible *qi* against identity politics. Now she sees natural, social, and even bodily relations as nothing else than "exotic interconnectedness," and the lyric subjectivity itself "an empty mirror in time," absorbing and reflecting that which still remains mysteriously outside. One copes with the continuing global desertification of mind and culture, not by keeping to the private, but by working through its cause and effect, its mechanisms. While in *The Desert Swimmer*, pure concepts radiate infinite rays into the experiential world, in *Footprints Wings Phantasms*, vitalistic, transformative words call for further explorations into the undefined yet glimmering parts of self and world. I am particularly amazed by the way my own phrases and images have crept into her poetic response and been transformed there, as if at last, I found a co-swimmer in this exciting, albeit dangerous, adventure in the "mythical ocean of Truth."

Incantation: Chant that produces magic or casts a spell.
Salubrious: Promoting health, well-being.
Speculate: Think contemplatively about various aspects of a given subject.
Qi: Flow of life-force energy.
Desertification: Process by which fertile land becomes desert.

Preface

By Kathryn Waddell Takara, PhD

In ***Footprints Wings Phantasms***, I seek to share my understanding that profound wisdom arises from experiencing transformative journeys along an elemental path to **awakening**. This book is my response to a deeply philosophical collection of poems, *The Desert Swimmer*, by Peter Dong Feng, PhD, a poet and professor at the University of Qingdao in China, where I gave lectures for seven summers. Feng's metaphors inspired me to create these reflective poems.

Everyone celebrates their high points and successes, but those in the process of **awakening** can also appreciate the right questions, efforts, and even failures, by stepping back, observing, accepting, and learning to fly. Due to hereditary and environmental tendencies—and the force of change—we have the capacity for whole creativity, but we live in a waking sleep amid shifting dimensions of confusion.

A new era is emerging. We have begun to recognize the potential of **awakening**. We are learning how individuals unite with the collective consciousness of energy exchanges. Surpassing both the self-centered "I love you" and the simply united yet inert "I am you," through process philosophy, we can envision possibilities: *traveling via paranormal non-locality; becoming others*; and *discovering infinity, the universal song of balance*.

Taking a leap of faith up into the often unobserved skies of subjectivity-plus-objectivity, I seek to present to people of all ages possibilities inherent in **awakening**. Each person must discover and develop constructive intentions. I affirm the creative balance among the forces of *yin* passivity, *yang* activity, and the transcendent third force. Recognizing phantasms, my poems explore metaphors like carefully walking, fearlessly flying, and falling into experiences.

In my youth, experiences of Jim Crow racism infused me with fear, dread, and courage. Through core teachings from my family, and gifts of strength and faith, I rebounded, seeking truth, justice, and goodness. Gaining insights while traveling internationally, I came to understand that life is always a transformative journey, a process enhanced by knowledge, by being present, and by the vital life force, *qi*.

Footprints Wings Phantasms challenges readers to be attentive to experiences. Transformation requires learning the value of "knowing thyself." Ever yearning to understand the great mysteries, I work to attain greater awareness of self and community. I aim to facilitate peaceful relations, by exploring the process of juggling the natural forces of naked freedom.

Awareness and detachment open possibilities for new ways of being. Through suffering, we can know the true joy of healing. As described by the mystic *San Juan de la Cruz*, in "the dark night," the soul travels through the influence of grace and undergoes purification of senses and spirit, before ascending the ladder of transformation. As we climb, knowledge and humility move us closer to enlightenment.

This collection tests traditional poetic boundaries by emphasizing a type of lyricism with hidden narratives about practice and process. The individual learns how to observe, direct, and accept change. Standing still does not result in growth. My readers are invited to fearlessly take flight—exploring organic life, self's shortcomings, and Nature's magical dance.

Join me on a breathtaking albeit sometimes terrifying journey to awaken both my conscience and my consciousness of life's transcendent order.

Footprints Wings Phantasms proposes a blueprint for how to encounter inevitable moments of fearlessly falling, and then flying up once more. Grateful for the insightful guiding footprints of teachers and fellow seekers, by embracing avatars of hope, we can soar.

With gratitude to many, I unveil this modest book, offering gifts of **awakening**.

Footprints Wings Phantasms

SECTION I
AWAKE

FALLING FROM THE SKY

Out of control
Empty, brimming, overflowing
Unsettled
Noodled in time
Weathered like winter.

TEARS OF THE MOON

Many I's and conflicts, being in China
Money bulging, explosions of buildings
Too many artificial tall landscapes
In new prospering cities
Replace historical continuities
Communities, *hutong*.
Gentrification.

Obsolete factories have fallen
Into crumbling disrepair
Replaced by elite resorts
For the rich and powerful.
Artworks and children's parks flourish.
Optimism.

Millions compete
Against self, against others.
Outreach diplomacy flies under my screen.
Commerce blares:
Leaders trade infrastructure for resources.
Unevenness.

Good fortune coins are forgotten
Communication lacking clarity
Ashes of translation
Familiar frustration.
Amnesia.

Slanderous wars
Rampant blight
Environmental decay
Abuse is acceptable/unacceptable.
Hypocrisy.

Twining vines tighten
Around the world of billions
Squeeze the political core of survival.
Loss.

Duplicitous ego persists
Invades all boundaries
Calls on power and resources
Tramples *Nature*, ignores respect of others.
Disgrace.

Tears of the moon fall in tall, long storms.

EXPOSURE

Naked
Falling from the sky
Diving into the *Sahara*
Where earth cradles desert
With four directions, four winds
Even four seasons . . . sometimes.

Crashing from the fiery west
Falling into watery identity
I fill with metallic fears
Another wounded swimmer
With cold skin, burning breath
Balancing *yin and yang*.

Called to silvery green islands
Challenging courage, I rise, I fly.

SEEING

Who are you?
An empty mirror in time.
Transnational histories reflect
Exotic interconnectedness
Discovered in a lyrical land
Of alluring transmissions.

TWISTERS OF FORTUNE

Mired in temporized ego
Pain and pleasure collude then collide.

The *Cheshire Cat* comedy
Plays out on a high branch of paradox
Conspires in altered-state observation.

Global alerts and warnings, tragic storms
Illusions, delusions, confusions invade
Politics.

Pollution contaminates life processes
Sandstorms, droughts, and plagues
Portend disaster.

Of twisted objectivity
I am a fortunate survivor.

NO COMMENT

Impressions can deceive.
What to see?
Navigate to where?
Sterile seeds to cure famine can kill.

No comment. No comment. No comment.

How to interpret the direction? Falling?
Flying?
Is there more to the eye
Than wounded survival?
How can one thrive and avoid negativity?
Shift the vision interior/exterior?

Engulfed in pride, permeated by passion
Surrounded in a simmering cauldron of loss
I see narcissistic dragonflies swarm above.
No answers, but maybe clarifying questions.

No comment.

ALL IS SPECULATION

Scientists sometimes solve riddles
Written in the sky
Neither wholly visible or invisible.

But false prophets, naysayers, and charlatans
Pretend to promote Justice.
They are pawns of deception.

Shades of color reconstruct reality
No remorse.
Politics move the momentum
Of clarity's mission
And fan the blinding dust to destruction.

Moon cycles and waters purify and transform:
Experimental interconnections
Mind/body/spirit
Visible and invisible battles of humans.

Excitement of complex rhythms
Strings of impressions
Compounds of sky and earth
Experiential uncertainties.
Speculations are both visible and invisible.

THE OTHERS

Disenfranchised minorities
Colonized, half- blinded, the powerless
Follow dark guides toward the unknown.
Throw the dice of Fate, seeking freedom.

Tomorrows surge from a fiery western sunset
Across the thirsty desert floor.
Flash floods surprise!
Flotsam and skeletons of lies
Swirl dangerously, produce
The polluted runoff of deceitful devilry.

Hope of homogeneity abandoned
The cosmic order disintegrates.
Embryos of harmony hide in discontent
disintegration—
Instead miscarriages, nightmares
Shards from broken dreams.

A few survive
Follow the promise of indigenous memories
Marvel at the trajectory of sun and moon.
Fueling, fulfilling essential needs and remedies
They reconcile destruction with resurrection.

LIBRA

Balance, thwarted, teeters
On the abyss of destruction, oblivion.
Blasphemy trumps Truth
Buried in the mausoleums of Justice.

Bones still firm float up
From the floods of *oubli*.
Ghosts and ghouls, wisps of promise
Blend in treacherous ochre smoke nearby.

Hope wants to control fragile feet and hands.
Justice sighs in a bottle, an empty cage.
Silence defeats a constellation of words
Weighed on an uneven scale
Darkness & light.

END OF THE RIVER

Red squabbles float down the muddy river
Past the jade shores of moon-flower vines
Twining around morning-glory surprises
Softening tense emotions.

I am many: I am you.
Bold, I am vitality personified
Ready for rapids and rocks
To brave depths and the unforeseen.

I experience uncontrollable gales
Illimitable torrents
And reach at last
The azure ocean of clarity.

FOREBODING

Death sits on my right shoulder
Foreboding . . .
Wrinkles, aches, episodes.

Propelled to transform confusion
I translate the hopes and fears of youth
Chew and swallow nuts and seeds
Of longing.

Healing discord, eating anger in stone soup
I implore, let my flow
Reach the end of the river
Merge together in promised peace
Out of time.

MORNING MEDITATION

A butterfly on the east wind
Wafts naturally
Attends a stunning sunrise
Invites celestial inspiration.

I sit and visualize
Gifts and harmonies of the morning
Contemplate the unexpected
Flight of a peacock to the rooftop
Countless *mejiro* in the avocado trees
And two `iwa birds circling
Over the *Pali* cliffs.

I chant affirmations of gratitude.
Love dances, dips, and lifts
Around the periphery of heartbeats
Rises above the soul-feast:
Paradise of *meum teum nostrum*.

FORCES UNLEASHED

Polar ice and glaciers crash
Into the Arctic Ocean.
Brooding hurricanes menace the horizon.
Swirling tornados lower to destroy.
Monsoons bully across the roiling seas.
Earthquakes and tsunamis proliferate.
Flaming forests reduce homes to ashes.

Nature leads us to recognize
Our insignificance.

Dark matter lingers from danger
Forebodes infinite holes of nothingness
Reveals traps
Pockets of self-abnegation.

Comparative paradox: eyes smart and wink.
Storms, disasters, and *vog*
Create surprising colorful sunsets.
Together we struggle with armies
Contradictions, temporal laws, processes
Tragicomedy of non-leaders and *Fake News*.

Wake up!

Work and explore the perennial riddles.
Find the keys to growth and survival.
Open the treasure chest of self-knowledge.

Beckon friends and gather memories
We still safe in relative seeing.
Help us to better understand community
Thoughts, emotions, and *Nature*.

Turn again toward the *North Star*
Hope veiled within.

SECTION II
EXPERIENCE

MIRROR FLOWER, WATER MOON

A bright copper coin in an indigo sky
The harvest moon reflects in my eyes.
In the cloudy mirror of me
I glimpse a shadow
Obliterated by the black face of night.

Ninety-six laws of confusion
Choke, blur, and blind transformation.
The muted moon is a beautiful woman,
Astarte.
Her bare shoulders glimmer.

In the watery mirror of light
Her nipples pose erect
Under her *bolero* blouse.
She illuminates the garden within
Finds magic
In the soft swinging skirt of palm trees.

Lunar light turns, dims, eats organic life
Attracts the attention of the dark ones.
The water moon feeds on the lunatic fringe
So says the esoteric legend of the *werewolf*.

LAND AND SAND

*C*hange direction, fly away, dare!

Travel light and take a stand.
Explore the unknown plains and valleys.

Seed the soul with love
Discovered in moonlight
Hidden within the ruby heart
Behind the navel, in the womb.

Breathe into the *Now*.
Awaken the *chakra*.
Brave searing sands
Camouflaged snakes and scorpions.

Seek golden retreat in the desert.
Find peace on the south wind's wings.

THE FALL

*C*rash through the sunset
With stunted wings, baggage-less
To the passionate place below the navel,
Root *chakra*, ocean of fertility.

Jolt to observation
Grounded and aware of measured movements
Mirrors empty of meaning and recognition.
Fight inertia and endless to-do lists
Messages of misunderstanding.

Scarlet garments trimmed in lace
Surreptitiously hide desire
Suggest a lack of self-control.

Grandma said:
Be in the *Now* of colorful potential.
Avoid cleverly hidden suits of imagination
Greedily stashed with pockets of money.
Step aside from trickery, trafficking, treachery.

Remember the escape to redemption
Despite wounded wings.

MOON MAGIC

Falling, flailing, flying
Naked and grasping
From the back of my head, I observe

Mind/ body/self and others
Flapping my wings to flee permanence
At the edge of eternal night.

I seek objectivity beyond hopes and fears.

Moon magic lights the path
Guides toward the mystical ocean of *Truth*.

PONDERING

Questions persist
In the land of evening charms.

Does the fish take the hook?
Does the nightingale fly and sing?

Where dwells compassion beyond self?

Waves crash on the soft sand
Kiss the glowing shores of communion.

MAMA'S LAP

Protected on Mama's lap
I crossed the highway at Green's Fork
Tuskegee, Alabama.
I witnessed fiery clannish rites
Mob mentality, rituals of terror.

I listened to Mama's voice
Heard her inspired intention
Reading me stories, fairy tales, verses
Comfortable on her favorite
Periwinkle blue upholstered chair.

Observing clear echoes of long-ago cultures
Mama educated her child
Explained fables, legends, myths—
Ali Baba, Aladdin, Scheherazade
Along with flawed leaders
Cleopatra, Hatshepsut, Solomon,
As well as goddesses and gods
Isis, Shiva, Shango
And lessons of great teachers
Jesus, Mohammad, Buddha, and more.

Mama taught protocols.
Enter in the eastern door, exit in the west

Honor the guest, respect others
Absorb wisdom, promote agency.

Sitting on Mama's lap, I learned to stay strong
Seek vibrancy, and healing change
Engage in learning, fly toward puzzling stars.

So much to remember and value!
Her instruction in my early youth
Mostly unrecognized, now cherished.

Experience

INQUIRIES

*L*istening to complex rhythms
Atonal chords ever-shifting
I ask, "Who are you?"
A presence diving, sinking, swimming . . .
What is your name?
What does it mean and to whom?
Questions abound
A quest for some unknown.

Why is the national agenda privileged?
Bigoted?
Why the bloody passport? Confiscated?
Can the emotions travel?
Understand another out of time?
What is your name? Who are you?"

Electronic relations flourish
Instead of flesh and eyes
Viruses, inadequate patches, police brutality.
Can this be justice?
What is your name?
Is there a link to lineage?
Is there a transcendent power for good?
Who are you?

WINGS OF *TRUTH*

Thou shalt pause.

Be aware of words, footprints, *phantasms*
Totems of the winged ones.

View grape-laden vineyards up the hillside.
Sip wines from a comfortable verandah.

Abundant harvest, prepared dishes, desserts
Thriving cultures produce variable recipes.

Verses are perched in the pearlescent clouds.

Below, civilizations rise and fall
Interminable histories and shipwrecks.
Rampant amnesia recycles *Truth*.

Thou shalt not trumpet fears and doubts.

Critics redouble
Seek fame and fortune.

Thou shalt mend the wings of essence.
 Discover philosophy, poetry, theology.
Invent new ideas and correspondences.
Breathe in the valley of *oubli*.
Boldly follow the path to the summit
Understanding all and nothing.

THE MECHANICAL SELF

Metallic clangs throb in the head
As chemical corruptions leech life
Poison the blood's precious roots.

Forget rum, whiskey, *Primo* beer.
Forget drugs, obsessions, violence.
Forget addictions, lies, accusations
Hazy conditions and pollution hangovers.

Reject the path of excess
The false dice flaming on the felt table.
Let go of crooked compulsions.
Recognize shifting kaleidoscopes
Transformative balance.

MEANDERING

Freed *intersectionality*.

Kimberlé Williams Crenshaw
Inspired the insight
Conceptualities.

Intersections chronicle solutions:
Service
Words
Seeing and understanding
Within a context of *Nature*.

Dancings toward democracy
Caught in razor crags
Deceptions invite illusions.

Connectivity conjures
Race and relationships
Women and history
Poetry and geopolitics.

YEARNING

𝕾tillness and movement
Aware of my solar plexus
The flow of *chi*

I hear memories
Recalling travels, treasured guests
Missing loving family, friends, pets.

Hybridity hints of intimate touchings
Tending the multiple gardens
Into the heart *chakra*.

I sense invasions
Hidden and frozen
Unspoken fears.

I taste perennial passings
Neglected aims . . .

Help comes from others.
Connect and catch up!
Go deep! *Stay woke!*

Responsible moments
So cherished—

I struggle to balance
Being and beyond

Giving, serving
Swimming in events and possibilities.

Experience

UNBIRTHED

*C*onstraints

No birthday, no birthmark, no markers
Body parts unacknowledged

Spirit

Despite reasonable defenses
Trapped in craters of silence

Lost

Unable to locate the hearth of intelligence
Impotent to articulate answers and meaning.

DESERT OF QUESTIONS

Who is the desert swimmer?
From windows stuck closed
By sand and old paint
Emanates a cacophony
Barely decipherable tones.

Who is playing a piano
Behind a dirty window?
Who is playing a guitar's seventh chord?

An interval inevitably appears
Silencing noisy confusion.

The mysterious *enneagram* offers answers
Symbol of evolution
Geometry of time and body types.

Surrounding the Earth Mother
Math and physics whisper
Future sonatas and requiems:
Life and fertility
Death and resurrection
Rites of passage
Sterile sands.

Dormant date seeds on the edge of an oasis
Are surrounded by drought
Where all is naught
When timelessness is everything
In the golden desert of questions.

SHOUT HALLELUJAH!

Gaia's diversity
Black women sing praise songs
Shout hallelujah, holler pain.

Adorned
With clapping bracelets of perception
Indigenous women whisper secrets
Collect herbs, stories, exercises *tantric*.

Unspeakable joys held in reflection
Women perennially silenced to invisibility
Hide their aging wanton womanhood.

Mysteries flutter nostalgic
Women camouflaged in plants and animals.
The pantheistic *Yoruba orisha* represent life:

Yemanja, mother of waters
Erzulie, goddess of love and women
Oshun, deity of generosity and sensuality.

Dream-shadows fly
With mercurial movements.
Women work hard, endure, shape-shift
Share food, rituals, whisper erotica.

Hidden meanings simmer
Beneath compassion and patience.
Secrets are stored deep in women's crevices.

From metaphorical eclipses and rebirths
Diverse messages transform longevity
Reveal recurrences and scales.

Women unveil the shadowed meaning
Beyond illusive words.
Truth of the feminine falls from the sky.

Experience

ORGASM OF HONEYBEES

Falling in spirals
Flying to love
Flowers thrill in the licking sun.

Winds in the tall garden caress.
Happiness buzzes the air
Punctuated by songs
Peacocks, dragonflies, and turtle doves.

Pagoda trees and peonies
Grow near the orange grove.

Who is picking and peeling the fruit?
Tending the crops?
Who is praying, dropping into sacredness?

The vineyards thrive.
Their wines are hearty and good.
Beneath sipping mouths, limbs tremble.

Energy throbs, strong in everything.
Sex is a distraction, a practice, a palliative
A necessity and elixir for youth and age

Melt into orgasm of honeybees.
Experience tastes of sweet being.
Let go and scream.

We, like stars, are made of fortified minerals
Light essential, creating elemental survival.

SEASONED FORGETFULNESS

ubli.

The north wind tears and screams
Behind closed, trembling doors
Harmonium shattered by darkened clouds.

The eye of time
Tempts, quivers, lies
Stays southern-biased in smoldering fires.

Imagination is a stepping stone
Up the eastern threshold
Across a bridge of unpredictable unknowns.

Down to the garden and harvest
Gather herbs and spices for cooking
To heal disease, digestion, and fears.

Forgotten tastes of sustenance
Raw/cooked, sweet/sour, bitter/salty.
Are birthed by Great Mother Earth

EXIT ON WINGS

Is there a dignified exit
From the labyrinth of life?

Remorse floats just beneath the thin skin of age.
Sincerity struggles: save self.
Enlighten conscience to forgiveness.
Individuation swallows the other.
Broken wings lack support.

Imagine an escape.
Expose procrastination.
Dig up abandoned aims.
Mend wings still weak with indecision.

Reconstruct the incomplete flight plan.
Correct disability of clipped wings.
Use reliable glue.

Follow ancient migrations, proven pathways.
Soar toward wholeness of *Truth*.
Seek the patterns of heaven.

Fly again toward salvation.
Fallible humans
We fail, fall back to earth.

Why bother?
What is a real exit?
How much are wings mendable?

Begin the search again.
New day, new moment, new efforts
To find flight's healing treasures:
Restoration, elusive love, and gratitude.

How much does false ego seek permanence?

SHIFTS OUT OF TIME

Flying over, wandering natural
Abstract soul-travel in a dream state
I's soar with fertile inspiration.

Shifting scales, recovered lineage
Expanding to alternative visions
To escape frantic disassociations.

Night ripples the sphere of exhaustion
While the moon's silver blanket
Heals the soul.

Double awareness fades in *andante* dreams.
Psychological practice grows transformative:
Shakespeare, Jung, Gurdjieff, Ouspensky.

Rise, float above the world's stage.

Visualize below—
Windows, doors, people diverse
In costumed dreams
Enticing, repelling, hiding.

Open, close, dismember reality.
Wake up!

Reconstruct.

Perspectives rise and sink.
Phantasms shift out of time.

SECTION III
UNDERSTAND

CHARMING

The architecture of words and breath
Celebrates our serendipitous meeting
In the *Sahara*'s oasis of poetry.

Connected in metaphors, we delight
Sharing naked art across time and space
Wings of words flapping and fluttering.

We create poems in colorful syllables
To facilitate/explicate/communicate
As best we can. Forever and ever. Amen.

ALL AND NOTHING

Winging up again
Beseeching answers in a clarion sky . . .

Help!

Currents of mysteries
Rush to the lake of understanding.

Jade dream-flowers float,
Drift, circle, and sink
Communing soundlessly with *Nature*.

Clarify freedom's possibility.
Inhale the true fragrance
Of night-blooming cereus and jasmine.

Words nurture the power of flight
All and nothing.

WINGS OF TRANSFORMATION

bserve.

Sad-looking wings
Barely stirring
Torn and tattered silhouettes
Rest low on a dull, weakened frame.

Wonder.

How to grow from nubs on scarred wings?
Choices to be made again
Tired, weak, and discouraged Seeker
Find a doctor! Where?
Verbal wings surge from within.

Look.

An epiphany hovers
On the ocean of awareness.
A friend offers repair, a serendipitous crossing.

Heal.

Gain new strength.
Practice with hope for harmony.

Head out once more
Toward the promising horizon
Illumined by a vibrant sunrise.

Celebrate.

The physician and the patient
Lift off at daybreak in gratitude
Soar to greet a bright continuance
Rise together
Accepting the miracle
Of restored wings and new flight.

TIMELESS CREATION

We must set out at dawn
Despite portending storms and frigid fears.

After the freeze of starry nights
Who dares to swim the scorching desert?

Shared aims propel interconnected artists
Inspire travel, conscience, twinkling creativity.

Day reveals the goddesses of sunny shores
And tranquil springs of pleasure.

Night exposes the gods of silver waters
Survival skills necessary, changing conditions.

Acknowledge *Cassiopeia*, the cosmic order
Varietal relations to space and time.

Lava and ice, cloudbursts and floods
Testify to the seasons of watery identity.

Recognize macro and micro notions.
Light a path to timeless creation.

ON THE MOVE

Floating once more to connections
Monitoring flights and abundant travel
Alabama, California, Hawai`i
Africa, Asia, Europe, Oceania

Adapting, experiencing excursions
Into *taiji, feng shui,* and *tantric yoga*
Morphing, dancing, and developing hind feet

Intuiting, falling while blind
Discovering the third eye
Seeing heaven beyond summits

Remembering ritualized conversations
Conversions angelic, rising and not
Gaia the mother and martyr in *Nature*

Flashing, challenging, moving, transforming
Rising and falling, stretching and shrinking
She sits still, voiceless and deaf, observing.

Proclamations of progress soar.
Beautiful and unfathomable, rooted, refreshed
Generational earth
Opens flight to the good soul.

ORBS

*A*t twilight

I'm falling, spiraling
From spirit-sky *orbs*
Toward the aesthetic ocean.

The stinging hot coastline
Reflects the crimson *phoenix* in my heart
Evoking pentatonic symphonies
And a desire for magical connections.

Bewitched by moon music
All night I dance in sapphire circles
Beside shadowy lakes and rivers
Twinkling hypnotic on cooling shores

Until the gradually coming aurora
Ever reflecting timeless orbs
Borrows light from father sun
Extinguishes mother moon.

The heavenly *orbs* astound:
Never the same rising
Never forgotten
Never abandoning life.

GOLDEN PHILOSOPHIES

Sun scrolls attention
In an unpredictably silent performance.
The third eye twitches with new possibilities.
A *phoenix* in me courts ancestral memories.

Venerated ancient leaders
Confucius, Plato, Gandhi, King
Acclaimed poets, prophets, teachers
Laozi, Du Fu, Rumi, Whitman.

Shadows of greatness
Fly and fall on a canvas of radiant light.
Intuitive recognition of shimmering moments
Deciphered, by whose standards?

Churches, temples, mosques
Show perennial hope.
Sacred texts promise eternal life.
Meditative messages transmit
Treasured instructions.

SUFI STORY

Hear the song of the butcher
The rhythm of his blade to the bone.

Substances of words rise
Bubbling in the cauldron.

They create a magic staccato
In the jumping pea soup.

Irrefutably tasty and original
The lamb flavors the boiling chickpeas.

Poetry evokes the capacity to cut
Eviscerate, cook, and transform.

Idioms can translate
Watery conditions into nourishing meaning.

Words transform like surrendering peas
Finally tender for the lover to digest.

VISIBLE AND INVISIBLE

Meet me in the jasmine garden
Under the long-leafed mango tree.

We can sip tea together
Write poems about *Taiyi*
And other intersections
Share impressions and essence.

We can honor sky, water, fiery deserts
Nurture the earth.

We can dissect history, appreciate philosophy
Ponder universal riddles.

Break the familiar sanctioned patterns
Be mindful of the adventures
With the desert swimmer.

Become fearless!

```
F                              RISING
 A
  L
   L              RISING
    I
     N
      G   RISING
```

IN A SOULFUL SKY

Witness collusions of day and night
Acknowledge the visible and invisible.

Meet me in the garden.
Smell the mangos and delight.

STRENGTH IN WORDS

Writers wordfully transform
Readers, knowledge, significance
Historical perceptions
Profound and deepening.

Writers expose forgotten footprints
Within the hurl to progress.

Writers discover essence
In stories, laughter, dreamtime
Among abandoned desks and chests.

Forgotten lives are hidden in journals
Old photos stored in secrets drawers
Histories dropped in pristine crystal vases
And in cracked and broken jars.

Writers dislodge words stymied in tongues
Stuffed in noses, throats, camouflaged *yoni*
Their meaning hidden
Behind earlobes and knees
In between fingers and toes.

Words reveal passages
To the womb and heaven.

The moon inspires
Sings a secret of feminine identity
Reflects fertility on earth's organic skin.

Understand

IS THERE A GREEN CALLING?

*B*e open to natural modes of flight
Amid the blind crowds and blighted earth
Stormy indecisions and fiery sunsets.

Ask boldly.
Make a request for emptiness.
Hear answers in the wind-stirred trees.

Observe the migrating birds, large and small
Flying toward persuasive forest adventures
Parroting the day
Alighting on shared branches.

ASTRAL EYES

I soar over malachite mountain cliffs
Weathered houses and fruit-laden gardens.

I dive to attention, surface to insights
Splash in the ever-churning sea of ideas.

I aim toward the *Sahara* of light
Observing *phantasms* of creative dreams.

Glossary

Aladdin – Character in folk tale known as "Aladdin and the Wonderful Lamp." A sorcerer disguised as a merchant gives a magic ring to a poor young man, recruiting him to find a magic lamp. Discovering the sorcerer's evil intent, he accidentally rubs the ring, which brings forth a supernatural genie (*jinn*), who helps the young man escape. His mother rubs the lamp while cleaning it, and another genie appears, who helps Aladdin become rich and marry a princess. The sorcerer steals the lamp. Helped by the ring genie, Aladdin kills the sorcerer and retrieves the lamp. The sorcerer's brother tries to take revenge, but Aladdin kills him, too. He inherits his father-in-law's position and becomes the Sultan. This tale does not originate from the original Arabic and Persian canon. Rather, it was introduced by a French translator, who claimed it had been told to him by Syrian storyteller in 1709. See ***One Thousand and One Nights***.

Ali Baba – Character in folk tale known as "*Ali Baba and the Forty Thieves*." Discovering that the magic words, "Open Sesame," open a cave where thieves have stored their plunder, Ali Baba, a poor woodcutter, takes a bag of gold, which changes his life. His greedy brother also finds the cave, but the thieves kill him. When they find out that Ali Baba has removed his brother's body to give him a funeral, they try to kill Ai Baba three times. Each time, his loyal slave woman, Morgiana, saves him, and as a reward he sets her free. When he tries again to kill Ali Baba, she kills the lead thief with a sword. In gratitude, Ali Baba allows her to marry his son. This tale does not originate from the original Arabic and Persian canon. Rather, it was introduced by a French translator, and the origin of the tale is unknown. See ***One Thousand and One Nights***.

Andante – Moderately slow tempo in musical compositions.

Astarte – Phoenician goddess most likely evolved from a Sumerian goddess, Innana/Ishtar, who appears more often in extant texts than any Sumerian deity. Not a mother goddess, she was depicted as a wife and mother. Like Innana/Ishtar, the Phoenician goddess Astarte represented fertility, sexuality, and war. She was represented with a star inside a circle that indicates the planet Venus, as well as the morning and/or evening star. Subsequently, the Greeks and Romans associated Astarte with Aphrodite, emphasizing love and procreation and disassociating her from war.

Astral – Of, connected with, or resembling the stars. The term sometimes encompasses paranormal or metaphysical phenomena.

Bolero – Short jacket without a fastened front that ends above the waist. This clothing style is attributed to Spain and Hispanic nations, popularized by the profession of bullfighting. With long, semi-long, or short sleeves, it is a popular modern style for women's blouses and dresses.

Buddha – (c. 563/480-483/400 BCE). Gautama Buddha, also known as Siddhārtha Gautama and Shakyamuni Buddha. He initiated the philosophy that became known as Buddhism, one of the world's major wisdom traditions. Most likely born and raised in eastern India, he was sheltered by his wealthy family. At age 29, he learned about the sufferings of ordinary people and began studying meditation. Rejecting asceticism, he believed one's duty is to help others. After arranging for the care of his wife and children, he became a homeless beggar. Meditating for 49 days under a fig tree (which came to be known as the Bodhi Tree), he achieved Enlightenment, becoming the Awakened One/Enlightened One. He continued traveling as a beggar, communicating his ideas like the Middle Way, the Eightfold Path, and the Four Noble Truths. His teachings, known as the Dharma, are that one should seek liberation from ignorance, desire, and hatred. By doing so, one can transcend the cycle of birth, suffering, and death—and achieve Nirvana.

Cassiopeia – Constellation in the sky named after a character of the same name in classical Greek mythology. The wife of the king of Phoenicia, she claimed herself and her daughter Andromeda to be more beautiful than the daughters of the Aegean sea-god Nereus. Angered by Cassiopea's vanity, the Greek sea-god Poseidon, who had defeated Nereus and assumed his powers, flooded the Phoenician protectorate of Ethiopia. An oracle advised Cassiopeia and her husband to sacrifice Andromeda to the sea, which they did, but the Greek hero Perseus rescued her. Poseidon punished Cassiopeia by placing her in the heavens tied to a chair as she had done to Andromeda. Year round, the constellation is visible from all latitudes north of 35°N. During late spring, it can be seen from all latitudes north of the Tropic of Capricorn.

Chakra – Sanskrit term for physical and metaphysical focal points in the body used in meditation techniques of the religions of India and other cultures. Related texts emphasize breathing practices, with *chakra* believed to connect with *nadi*, energy channels. *Chakra* are associated with Hinduism, Jainism, Buddhism—and with *kundalini* yoga. Buddhist texts usually mention four *chakra*, while Hindu texts usually have seven. It should be noted that theory and practice of *chakra* differ greatly from the Chinese system of meridians followed in acupuncture.

Cheshire Cat – Character in the 1865 novel *Alice's Adventures in Wonderland* by British author Charles Lutwidge Dawson under the pen name Lewis Carroll. A girl named Alice falls into a garden rabbit hole and finds herself trapped in a world of fantastic creatures, including the Cheshire Cat. Theorizing on Carroll's inspiration, some point to a cat's face carved on the church tower in his hometown where his father was the minister. Others observe that, during Carroll's youth, a cat's face appeared on a popular brand of Cheshire cheese. The Cheshire Cat character appears repeatedly in Carroll's book, notably in the scene where the King and Queen of Hearts condemn it to death by beheading—but the cat has materialized without its body. Confused, the dictators debate whether or not they can behead a disembodied head.

Cleopatra VII – (69-30 BCE). From when Alexander the Great of Greece invaded Egypt circa 323 BCE until the deposing of Cleopatra VII by the Romans in 30 BCE, the Ptolemy dynasty ruled Egypt. Ptolemy and Cleopatra were popular names in the incestuous royal family. Cleopatra VII's uncle, born to a lesser wife of his father, was not in line to inherit the throne, but unexpected deaths led to his being named the pharaoh. To hold his power, he paid bribes and murdered relatives. He appointed his young niece, Cleopatra VII, as his co-regent. He ruled Egypt until his death at age 38.

Confucius – (551-479 BCE). Also known as Kong Fuzi, from which the Western name, Confucius, derives; by his birth name, Kong Qiu; as well as by the honorific names Zhongni and Kongzi. He was a philosopher, teacher, editor, politician, and leader of the Spring and Autumn periods of Chinese history. His philosophy emphasized personal and governmental morality, correctness of social relationships, justice, and sincerity. Following the victory of the Han over the Chu after the collapse of the Qin, Confucius' thoughts received official sanction and developed into a system known as Confucianism. His principles had a basis in common Chinese tradition and belief. He championed strong family loyalty, ancestor worship, and respect for elders by children and for husbands by wives. He recommended the family as a basis for ideal government. He espoused the well-known principle "Do not do to others what you do not want done to yourself," which is similar to the Golden Rule in the West.

Crenshaw, Kimberlé Williams – (b. 1959). United States legal scholar, critical race theorist, and civil rights advocate. Originally from Ohio, she holds degrees from Cornell University and the University of Wisconsin, as well as a J.D. from the Harvard University Law School. Having clerked for Wisconsin Supreme Court Judge Shirley Abramson and teaching at UCLA Law School, today Crenshaw is a full professor at Columbia Law School. She authored the 2001 background paper for the United Nations World Conference on Racism and has published influential books including *Black Girls Matter*, *Mapping the Margins*, and *Intersectionality*. To feminist theory, Crenshaw is credited with introducing *intersectionality*, in which interwoven factors affect a matrix.

Du Fu – (712-770). Poet-sage of China's Tang Dynasty, who wrote about history, morality, and sensitive feelings for humanity.

Enneagram – In philosophy and psychology, a description in nine interconnected personality types of the conscious and unconscious human mind known as the psyche. Around 1954, Oscar Ichazo introduced the concept of the enneagram as nine ways that the ego in early life becomes fixated with the psyche. Around 1949, P. D. Ouspensky published a diagram of a nine-pointed model of stages in any complete process, crediting G. I. Gurdjieff for introducing the model to study groups in Russia in 1916. Scholars hypothesize various origins. One theory dates it to a 4th century Christian mystic, another to the Pythagorean *tetractys*, and still others to Sufi Muslim origins. While Gurdjieff is widely credited for making the figure widely known (the Fourth Way Enneagram), it was Ichazo who coined the term "Enneagram of Personality" and conceived the nine personality types. The enneagram is also connected with a theory of body types, personalities being influenced by the lymph glands and circulation from one point to the next. Each type manifests a fairly predictable behavior pattern associated with a body type. See **Mechanical Self**, **Gurdjieff**, and **Ouspensky**.

Erzulie Freda – In Haitian Vodou, there are several spirits with names containing Erzulie. Vodou, which originated in Nigeria among West African slaves. Forced to convert to Christianity, West African slaves adapted a variety of African religious practices with Roman Catholicism and European mysticism. Carried by slaves, Vodou took root in Haiti. Bondye (God) is believed to be unreachable, so Vodouisants pray to spirits known as *loa*, classified into 21 spiritual "nations" and also grouped by family. *Loa* of the Erzulie family reside in the "nations" of Rada, Petro, and several others. In Rada, the *loa* called Erzulie Freda is the flirtatious, and sometimes vain, goddess of love who sheds tears of regret and longing. She is syncretized with the long-suffering Virgin Mother figure, Our Lady of Sorrows. Erzulie Freda also represents love, beauty, jewelry, dancing, luxury, and flowers. She wears three wedding rings, one for each husband. Her symbol is a heart. Erzulie Freda stands for femininity and compassion, yet can also embody jealousy, spoiledness, and laziness. During ritual possession, she enters both male and female bodies, flirting and seducing.

Fake News – Propaganda style of misinformation that dates back to the ancient world. In the United States, during the 2016 presidential election, Fake News played a significant role. Many of the fake stories originated in Macedonia, where young entrepreneurs planted and perpetuated false stories about the candidates to make money by driving traffic to their internet publications. The Russian government is also considered a leading source of fake news. After his inauguration, President Donald J. Trump adopted the term, using it to attack and discredit leading media organizations by accusing them of publishing falsehoods.

Feng shui – Chinese philosophical system dating from the Tang Dynasty. *Feng* means wind/breath with *yang* energy, representing health. *Shui* means water with *yin* energy, conveying prosperity. The system aims to maximize harmony to enhance good social relations. It applies the principles of the four directions, the north-south axis, and the five elements. It is used in design and architecture, including placement of doors, gates, homes, guests, plazas, temples, and tombs. It uses a system of divination to enhance the flow of material energy, *qi*. See ***qi.***

Gaia – In Greek mythology, this goddess personifies the Earth. One of the Greek primordial deities, Gaia is the ancestral mother of all life: the primal Mother Earth. Her equivalent in the Roman pantheon was Terra.

Gandhi, Mahatma – (1869-1948). Birth name Mohandas Karamchand Gandhi. He was an Indian philosopher, attorney, civil-rights activist, animal-rights supporter, author, and advocate for nonviolent resistance, truth, and democracy. He participated in the struggle against apartheid in South Africa, and he led the independence movement against colonial British rule, which created the nations of India, Pakistan, and Bangladesh. Gandhi envisioned locally based, self-sustaining economies.

Gurdjieff, George Ivanovich – (1866-1949). Philosopher, musical composer, spiritual/mystical teacher, and author. Of Greek-Armenian heritage, he taught that most humans do not possess a unified mind-emotion-body consciousness, living in a hypnotic state of "waking sleep." He believed that it is possible to transcend to a higher state of consciousness and achieve full human potential. He called this awakening practice the Work (as in, "work on oneself"), the Method, and the Fourth Way. His books include *The Herald of Coming Good* and his trilogy *All and Everything*. See **enneagram**, **Mechanical Self**, and **Ouspensky**.

Hafiz – (1315-1390). Also Romanized as Hafez. Khwāja Shams-ud-Dīn Muḥammad Ḥafeẓ-e Shīrzī. Lyrical poet considered the greatest Persian author, his poetry was famous in the Islamic world during his life. First translated into English in 1771, his theosophical works have influenced numerous authors. The epigraph on page ix comes from his poem "A Crystal Rim," in The Gift: Poems by Hafiz, the Great Sufi Master, translated by Daniel Ladinsky (New York: Penguin, 1999: 49).

Hatshepsut – (c. 1507–1458 BC). Fifth pharaoh of the 18th Dynasty. Hatshepsut is believed to have ruled Egypt for about 21 years. Following the death of her husband and half-brother, the pharaoh Thutmose II, she became co-regent in the name of their young son, Thutmose III, but she achieved her own power, claiming that she was actually the legitimate intended heir of her father, Thutmose I. She established numerous trade networks and construction projects, and her reign was generally peaceful and extremely prosperous. Her influence in art and architecture was so consequential that many of the surviving ancient Egyptian artifacts depict her.

Hutong – Neighborhoods in China formed by clusters of narrow streets or alleys running along lines of traditional courtyard residences. They are commonly located in northern Chinese cities, most prominently in Beijing. Since the mid-20th century, many *hutong* have been demolished to make way for new roads and buildings. Some *hutong* have been designated as protected areas in an attempt to preserve this aspect of Chinese cultural history.

Hybridity – Theories in biology, linguistics, cross-cultural studies, post-colonial theory, migrant literature, and intercultural theatre. *Hybridity* means mixture, from *hybrid*, something that is mixed. In the West, the term dates back to classical times, when the term was used in agriculture. It was also applied to racial mixing, mainly in terms of Greek disapproval of interbreeding with non-Greeks, and Roman disapproval of interbreeding with non-Romans. Mikhail

Bakhtin applies the *hybridity*-associated term *polyphony* to folklore and anthropology.

Intersectionality – See **Crenshaw**.

Isis – Ancient Egyptians worshipped deities based on mythological tales. The most influential and elaborate myth, the tale of Osiris, originated around the 24th century BCE. The god and king Osiris is murdered and torn apart by his brother, Set, who steals his throne. His wife, the goddess Isis, reassembles and reanimates his body, and they conceive their son Horus, who eventually overthrows his uncle, completing his father's resurrection. The Osiris myth emphasizes proper succession of kingship, order over disorder, and a symbolic afterlife. Isis was believed to assist the dead in entering the afterlife, and she was considered a divine mother figure. She became one of the most important Egyptian deities, and her cult spread widely throughout the Greek and Roman worlds. Originally known as Aset or Eset, which means "throne," Isis is her Greek name. A feminine archetype for creation, she became a goddess of fertility, healing, and motherhood.

`Iwa – Scientifically known as Frigata Minor, this type of seabird is also called the great frigate bird. Their beaks are blue and gray, and in adulthood their plumage is mostly black. They nest in remote islands and tropical areas with lush vegetation, such as the Northern Hawaiian Islands. Consummate fliers, they quickly soar, turn, and dive for fish. Although their diets consist mainly of fresh fish, they occasionally steal food from other birds by forcing them to regurgitate their catches. Thus, their Hawaiian name, `Iwa, means "thief."

Jesus – (c. 4 BCE – 30/33 CE). Central figure in the religion of Christianity. Nearly all antiquity scholars agree that, historically, the person known as Jesus existed. They disagree on the historical reliability of the Gospels. They also disagree about the resemblance of Jesus as depicted in the New Testament to the historical Jesus. The Gospels of Mark, Matthew, Luke, and John describe Jesus as a teacher and healer who gathered followers among and beyond his native region of Judea. After the Roman prefect Pontius Pilate executed him, some of Jesus' followers attested that they saw him risen from the dead and that they had witnessed his resurrected self ascend into heaven. Tales about and sayings by Jesus passed throughout the Roman world. Compiled in various versions, they became the Gospels. After Jesus' crucifixion, a Greek-educated and Roman-employed Jewish soldier named Paul, also Saul, who had been ordered to kill followers of Jesus, reported that he had a vision of Jesus while traveling from Jerusalem to Damascus. Paul dedicated his life to teaching that Jesus is the Jewish Messiah, the Son of God come to save the world. According to the Book of Acts, the term "Christians" originated with Paul's outreach to a community in Antioch, and much of the New Testament consists of Paul's letters to early Christian groups. After the Roman Emperor Constantine (c. 208-337 CE) converted to Christianity, the religion ceased to be persecuted in the Roman Empire. Christianity survived the Dark Ages and spread throughout Europe and other regions. Today, Christianity is the most populous world wisdom tradition, with more than 30% of the earth's population. Islam, which recognizes Jesus as a great prophet, is the second-largest at more than 25%. Contemporary mysticism embraces Jesus as the incarnation of a higher state of consciousness that can lead each human being to fulfill one's spiritual potential.

Jung, Carl Gustav – (1875-1961). Psychiatrist and psychoanalyst who founded analytical psychology. From Switzerland and with German ancestry, he grew up in a family in which his father eked out a living as a Swiss Reformed pastor and his mother was a housewife who suffered from mental illness. Experiencing anxiety attacks, he read widely, learning about neuroses. He entered medical school and, despite his father's death, with the help of relatives, graduated and began working in a mental hospital. He married a wealthy young woman, Emma Rauschenbach, who despite his extramarital affairs loved him unreservedly and worked as his dedicated research assistant until her death in 1955. In his youth, Jung contacted 50-year-old Sigmund Freud, who was already familiar with his writing, and they cooperated professionally for six years. During WWI, while Jung was a Swiss Army doctor, they abruptly ceased their mutual research based on divergent opinions on the field of psychology. Whereas Freud emphasized repressed desires resulting during early sexual development, Jung held that the collective unconscious inherited from ancestors was the key to the development of personality. Jung did not escape his mother's legacy. He reported seeing hallucinations from an early age, and after the break with Freud he heard voices and saw visions, worrying that he might be experiencing schizophrenia. Determined to get at the root of the problem, for sixteen years, Jung kept a journal with his writings and drawings that he called the *Red Book*. During this time, he developed his ideas about archetypes of the collective unconscious. His work has influenced psychiatry, anthropology, archaeology, philosophy, religious studies, literature, and folklore.

King, Martin Luther, Jr. – (1929-1968). Leader of the nonviolent civil rights movement against Jim Crow laws in the United States. As African Americans in Atlanta, Georgia, his father and mother struggled against prejudice and discrimination. His father was a Baptist minister, and his mother was an active principal member in the congregation. Following in his father's footsteps, King also became a Baptist minister. He earned a BA in Sociology, a BDiv, and a PhD in theology. In 1953, he married Coretta Scott, who, like his mother, worked hand-in-hand alongside her husband in his work, and they had four children together. In 1955, King emerged as a leader in the Montgomery Bus Boycott that challenged segregation laws separating "white" from "colored" in public transportation. In 1957, he became a charter member of the Southern Christian Leadership Conference. Writing prolifically, King led many marches for desegregation, the right to vote, labor rights, and other rights. In 1963, he was arrested for the 13th time (he would be arrested 39 times), when he wrote his influential *Letter from Birmingham Jail*. Later that year, he led the March on Washington for Jobs and Freedom, at which he delivered his famous "I Have a Dream" speech. Even after Congress passed the Civil Rights Act of 1964 and Voting Rights Act of 1965, King continued leading efforts for justice, advocating for equal housing rights, against the Vietnam War, and for help for poor Americans of all colors. In the spring of 1968, he traveled to support a strike by sanitation workers in Tennessee, where he was assassinated by a stalker who shot him. It was not the first attempt on his life. A few years earlier, another stalker had stabbed him. King is revered for his role in the advancement of civil rights using the tactics of nonviolence and civil disobedience based on his Christian beliefs and inspired by the nonviolent activism of Mahatma Gandhi.

Laozi – (d. 531 BC). Chinese writer and philosopher believed to have authored the *Dao De Jing* (also Romanized as Tao Te Ching). The book is a commentary of the nature of existence, offering balanced moral and spiritual guidance and concerned with working for the good of humanity. The book speaks of the need to be flexible and observant, addressing the four virtues of reverence/respect, sincerity, gentleness, and service/supportiveness.

Libra – The seventh of twelve astrological signs in the zodiac established about the 5th century BCE in ancient Babylon. Around the 4th century BCE, the Babylonian zodiac entered Greek astronomy, with the earliest extant Greek text on the subject authored circa 190 BCE. Claudius Ptolemy (c. 90-168 BCE) popularized the twelve-sign system for astronomy and astrology, and his *Almagest* remained an influential text for 1,000 years. In Babylonia astronomy, Libra was associated with scales and balance, as well as with the claws of the scorpion. In classical Greece, Libra was symbolized by the goddess Themis, who held the Scales of Justice. Libra came to represent civility, fairness, and law. Libra is the only zodiac constellation represented by an inanimate object, the scales. The other eleven signs denote animals or mythological characters. In ancient Chinese astronomy and astrology, the constellation known in the West as Libra is known as the Azure Dragon of the East (Dong Fang Qing Long), while the name of the Western constellation is rendered in Chinese as the Celestial Steelyard Constellation (Tian Cheng Zuo). Libra is one of the three zodiac air signs, the others being Gemini and Aquarius.

Mechanical Self – G. I Gurdjieff and his student P. D. Ouspensky developed and elaborated on a system of spiritual development known as the Fourth Way. They identified and incorporated three major paths of spiritual mastery: fakirs over the physical body, monks over the emotions, and yogis over the mind. Via the Fourth Way, one knows that the mechanical self is the default position of the human person. In a waking sleep, we believe that we regularly exercise free will, true consciousness, and freedom—but we rarely do. Throughout our lives, we do almost everything mechanically, without thinking. Gurdjieff and Ouspensky advocated attentiveness: waking up to one's behavior. Inattentiveness comes from imitated thoughts, behavior, and actions, influenced by expectations of family, community, culture, trends, and the desire to fit in. Those are natural desires—and truly wonderful when we are attentive to them—such as imitating the actions of a good boss when supervising subordinates, or preparing a good meal with family and friends. Inattentively, we can hurt others. We speak without thinking. We act without considering even our own good interests. Revisiting central concepts while developing the body, emotions, and mind is key to the Fourth Way. See **enneagram**, **Gurdjieff**, and **Ouspensky**.

Meijiro – Small perching bird known as Zosterops Japonicus, also called Japanese White-Eye. It nests across East Asia, such as in China, Japan, Korea, the Philippines, Taiwan, and Vietnam. Its name in Japanese is Meijiro, where historically these birds were kept caged. It has been introduced into other places, for example into Hawai`i in 1929, where Meijiro have proliferated and are adversely affecting populations of native birds.

Meum teum nostrum – In Latin, literally, "me you we." This phrase derives from the poem "The Thieves" by the Irish-British author Robert Graves, also known as Robert von Ranke Graves (1895-1985). Graves was an expert in Celtic history and Irish mythology—and a poet, as well as a novelist and critic. His celebrated love poem "The Thieves" begins, "Lovers in the act dispense / With such meum-teum sense." The first stanza ends, "And their nostrum is to say: / I and you are both away." In the second stanza, the *I* and the *you* separate and reunite. The third stanza proposes that lovers can be so enamored with each other that they can forget their responsibilities to life and others.

Muhammad – (570 CE-8 June 632 CE). Muhammad ibn `Abdullah ibn `Abdul-Muttalib ibn Hāshim. Founder of the religion of Islam, considered the final Prophet of God by all the main branches of Islam. Born in Mecca and orphaned at a young age, he became a merchant. At age 25, he married a 40-year-old widow and businesswoman, Khadija. For the next 24 years, she was his only wife. (After her death, he married further wives, often rescuing them from social ostracization.) In 605 CE, during a renovation of the spiritually revered, ancient Kaaba structure, the Prophet resolved a dispute regarding who should carry the venerated Black Stone back to its place on its eastern corner. At this time, Arab religions were predominantly polytheist, although monotheist Jews shared oral traditions with Arabs, as did Christians, who had become an established minority in Arabia. For several weeks a year, the Prophet prayed alone in a cave. In 609 CE, the Angel Gabriel visited him in the cave, compelling him to commit to memory oral verses that would become part of the Quran, the holy book of Islam. Unnerved yet unafraid, he devoted more time to prayers. After three years, the angel visited him again, commanding him to begin reciting the verses. He had revelations for the rest of his life. Listening to him recite, his followers memorized and passed on the verses to others. The written version of the Quran was compiled in Arabic by his scribe Zayd ibn Thabit. The Quran, which has stories and sayings in common with the Hebrew and Christian Bibles, advocates monotheism. Adherents of Islam, known as Muslims, agree that, along with Judaism and Christianity, Islam is an Abrahamic religion. The Quran mentions many prophets, including David, Solomon, and Jesus. However, Muslims believe that the Prophet was the final Prophet of God. More than merely a religious figure, the Prophet was also a political and military leader who united Arabia. Following his death, disagreement arose over who his successor should be: his friend and compatriot Abu Bakr, or his cousin and son-in-law Ali ibn Abi Talib. Generally speaking, today's Sunni Muslims follow the Abu Bakr legacy, whereas Shia Muslims follow the Ali ibn Abi Talib legacy. Sufis approach Islam from a mystical-ascetic approach, emphasizing personal experience with God.

Nature – Nature spelled with a capital N alludes to spirituality, cosmic laws, and fixed processes existing in every living thing.

One Thousand and One Nights – Collection of Middle Eastern folk tales collected between the 8th and 14th centuries, with roots in Arabic, Greek, Indian, Jewish, and Persian cultures.

Orb – Ancient and medieval thinkers like Plato, Aristotle, Ptolemy, and Copernicus considered celestial bodies to be like jewels embedded in various heavenly spheres. These spheres were called epicycles or orbs, believed to rotate above the earth. Today, an orb (called an orbit) is considered to be the path that a planet follows as it rotates around its sun; the path that a sun follows as it rotates through its galaxy; and the path that a galaxy follows as it rotates through the universe. An orb/orbit is any spherical path followed by a smaller body around a larger body.

Orisha – In the Yoruba religion, entities that reflect aspects of and serve as intermediaries for the divine creator and energy source, Olodumare, also called Olorun. Formed of diverse traditions, Yoruba religion is associated with the Itan, which consists of a body of songs, histories, stories, and other cultural concepts uniting Yoruba society. The religion holds that every human must become united with Olodumare. Between the 16th to the 19th centuries, during the Atlantic slave trade, Yoruba were brought as slaves to the Americas, and their descendants preserved aspects of the Yoruba religion, which teaches that a person proceeds through a series of life-and-death cycles, evolving toward transcendence. An individual should engage in prayer through meditative recitation and sincere veneration, which produces joy. See **Oshun**, **Shango**, **Yemoja**, and **Yoruba**.

Oshun – One of the *orisha* in the Yoruba religion. The second wife of the male *orisha* known as Shango, she embodies the feminine attributes of beauty, gracefulness, and sensuality. She is appealed to for matters relating to fertility, the health of babies, and female disorders. Cool, flowing water is said to be her healing method. Practitioners pray to her for clarity. See **Orisha**.

Oubli – French noun that means "forgetfulness, oversight, or omission." It is derived from the French verb *oublier*, to forget (something), or to leave something behind accidentally. It is related to the French adjective *oublieux*, oblivious, forgetful, failing to remember.

Ouspensky, Pyotyr Demianovich – (5 March 1878 - 2 October 1947). Philosopher and author. Born in Moscow, Russia, in 1907, while working for a newspaper, he began a lifelong study of Theosophy, an esoteric, mystical Christian belief founded in the 1500's that ancient wisdom can illuminate direct knowledge of divinity. In 1909, Ouspensky published *The Fourth Dimension*, exploring complex mathematical concepts. In 1912, he published his second book, *Tertium Organum*. In 1913, Ouspensky traveled to India, Sri Lanka, and Egypt to seek theosophical wisdom. When WWI began, he returned to Moscow, where he met G. I. Gurdjieff in 1915. They studied together and planned to open a school. After the Russian revolution, Ouspensky traveled to Istanbul. By the 1920's, his works had gained international notice, and he was invited to lecture in London. In 1922, Gurdjieff established the Harmonious Development of Man Institute in France. In 1924, Ouspensky decided their ideas were too dissimilar, so he broke with Gurdjieff and founded his own institute, the Society for the Study of Normal Psychology (known today as The Study Society) in London. In the 1920's and 1930's, Ouspensky influenced many British authors, including Aldous Huxley and T. S. Eliot.. Published posthumously in 1947, Ouspensky's book *In Search of the Miraculous*, published by Ouspensky's widow with Gurdjieff's approval, discusses some of Gurdjieff's teachings. In 1957, Ouspensky's students published a collection of his lectures, entitled *The Fourth Way*. See **ennegram, Gurdjieff, Mechanical Self**.

Pali Cliffs – Facing the northeast coast of the island of O`ahu in the US State of Hawai`i are the Windward cliffs of the Ko`olau mountain range. A portion of these cliffs known for its natural beauty and panoramic views is called the Nu`uanu Pali, or simply the Pali. In 1959, the Pali tunnels were bored into the mountainside, connecting downtown Honolulu with the Windward side of the island, a route known as the Pali Highway.

North Star – The brightest star in the sky also called Polaris. It is found in the constellation of Ursula Minor, also known as the Little Dipper. Because it lies in a direct line in the Earth's axis, it is commonly used for navigation.

Phantasm – Figment of the creative imagination. An illusion or apparition. An illusory likeness of something.

Phoenix – In classical Greek legends, a mythical bird associated with the sun that cyclically regenerates or is reborn in some other way. It was said to live 500 years before dying and being born again. It was described as surrounded by a halo from which rays emanate, and associated with the colors red and yellow. The bird symbolized renewal. One ancient writer compared it to a rooster. The Greek phoenix must be distinguished from the Chinese *fenghuang*. Even though the *fenghuang* was also a mythical bird whose name meant "rooster" and although westerners have referred to it as a "phoenix," the *fenghuang* differed significantly from the Greek phoenix. It was considered to be a composite of many birds, with feathers of the five fundamental colors: black, white, red, green, and yellow. Originally, *feng* was thought to be the male manifestation of this bird, with *huang* being the female, the *fenghuang* was thought to represent the ultimate union of *yang* and *yin*. It symbolized virtue and grace.

Plato – (c. 428-348 BCE). Philosopher of classical Greece and founder of the Athens Academy, the first institution of higher learning in the west. He is considered the founder of philosophy in the western tradition. He was a student of Socrates, writing in dialectical dialogues about his teacher's ideas—and his own—about philosophy, ethics, politics and law, metaphysics, and epistemology. A teacher himself, one of Plato's own students was Aristotle. All of Plato's works are considered to have survived. Contemporary scholars believe that a number of works attributed to him were authored by others. Plato's theory of form argues thateverything imitates an ideal form of that thing. For instance, there are many types of trees, but only one ideal form of a tree on which all the others are based.

Primo – Primo Brewing Company is a Honolulu-based beer brewing company now owned and operated by Pabst Brewing Company. Its brand is known as "Hawai`i's original beer."

Qi – Flow of life-force energy. Also Romanized as *chi*. The concept is used in Chinese martial arts and *feng shui*. In *feng shui*, it applies to the orientation of a structure, its age, and its interaction with the surrounding environment, including local microclimates, slope of the land, vegetation, and soil quality. See ***feng shui***.

Qingdao – Also Romanized as Tsingtao. Qingdao, located in Shandong Province, is one of China's major coastal cities, formerly known for its sanatoriums for those suffering from tuberculosis because of the good quality of the air and temperate climate. In Chinese, *qing* is "cyan" or "greenish-blue," and *dao* is "island." During WWI and WWII, the area was occupied first by the Germans and then by the Japanese. In 2014, Qingdao had a population of nearly 10 million. Located on the Yellow Sea, Qingdao is a major seaport, naval base, and industrial center. Its Jiaozhou Bay Bridge is the world's longest sea bridge, and the city hosts the second-largest brewery in China, the Tsingtao Brewery.

Rumi – (1207-1273). Mowlānā Jalālodin Balkhi. Known in Persia as Jalāl ad-Dīn Muhammad Balkhī. Known in the West as Rumi. He was descended from Islamic jurists and theologians, many of whom were Sufi mystics, including his father. He was born into a Persian-speaking family in what is now Afghanistan, in an area where Sufism had developed for several centuries. Between 1215 and 1220, escaping Genghis Khan, his father moved their family and some of his students westward toward Baghdad, Hejaz, Mecca, and Damascus. Entering Turkey, they settled for seven years in Karaman, where his mother and brother died. In 1228, the group moved to Konya. His father led a madrassa school there and passed his scholarly role to his son. For nine years until about 1241, Rumi studied under a major Sufi teacher. He became an Islamic jurist in Konya, delivering sermons, issuing *fatwa*, and teaching. A famous Sufi dervish became his teacher, but disappeared and was presumed dead. Bereft, Rumi poured his grief into his mystical poetry collection *Divan-e Shams-e Tabrizi*. A student became his scribe for twelve years. The result was a six-volume poetry collection, M*asnavi*. Rumi produced works in many genres and led the community of his family and students. His writing shows that while he took his Islamic faith seriously he welcomed those of other faiths into friendship with Muslims, freely, without reservation. The mysticism of his poetry is said to penetrate the human soul. His poems have been translated into many languages and in various formats. Rumi is the most popular and best-selling poet in the United States.

Sahara – Largest hot desert in the world. It consists of more than three million square miles, bordered by the Red Sea to the east, the Mediterranean Sea to the north, the Atlantic Ocean to the west, and the Sahel tropic savannas to the south. Hyperarid, with sparse vegetation, it covers much of North Africa. During the day, some parts can reach more than 176 ° F (80 °C). The region's languages consist mainly of Arabic dialects, along with variants of Berber and Beja.

Scheherazade – Character who narrates of the compilation of folk tales known as *One Thousand and One Nights*. The legend about her, which frames the collection, begins with a fictional Persian king who, to prevent any wife from betraying him, marries a new wife daily, murdering her the next morning. Scheherazade, the daughter of one of his ministers, is a brilliant scholar and historian. She volunteers to become his wife, telling him an elaborate story until dawn. Because she ends on a cliffhanger, he grants her a reprieve. After 1,001 nights of stories, she stops. He spares her, transformed into a wise king. See ***One Thousand and One Nights.***

Shakespeare, William – (1564-1616). English poet, playwright, and actor. He is considered the greatest writer in the English language and the greatest dramatist who ever lived.

Shango – One of the *orisha* in the Yoruba religion. Prior to his posthumous deification, he was the third Alafin (king) of the Oyo Kingdom, with three wives: Oshun, Oba, and Oya. He is associated with anger, justice, thunder, and drumming. Shango worshippers venerate rocks and stones that have been created by lightning strikes. See **Orisha** and **Yoruba**.

Shiva – One of the three principal deities of Hinduism, along with Brahma and Vishnu. Hinduism developed from a variety of Indian wisdom traditions. Between 1500 and 600 BCE, during the Vedic period, Indo-Aryan peoples migrated from the south, establishing an agricultural society and later urbanized states. Worship consisted of sacrifices accompanied by chants, songs, and prayers. The Vedic chants transmitted an oral tradition that emphasized production of spiritual sounds while relating ethical tales. Because every living thing undergoes *samsara* (rebirth), which is affected by *karma* (consequences for actions), through *yoga* (paths/practices), one may attain transcendence. In the major sect of Hinduism known as Shaivism, Shiva is believed to be the Supreme Being or to be the soul/self (Atman) within every being. Shiva is considered both a destroyer of evil and a transformer of the universe. Its followers sometimes interweave Shivism with Shaktism. Shaktism holds that metaphysical reality is feminine, led by the supreme Devi, who embodies the cosmos, and who is accompanied by other goddesses. Because Shaktism rejects dualisms, the feminine and masculine are twin aspects of the divine universe.

Solomon – One of the kings of Israel, said to have reigned from 970 to 931 BCE. Succeeding his father,

King David, he was wealthy and powerful. He is discussed in the Hebrew Bible (where he is also called Jedidiah) and the Quran (where he is called Sulayman). He is described as a wise ruler yet one who committed grievous social and religious sins. He is credited with building the First Temple in Jerusalem, dedicating it to Yahweh, the God of Israel.

Stay woke! – Modern urban slang phrase emphasizing the need for an individual to keep oneself informed about incomplete and/or inaccurate media coverage, primarily regarding governmental deprivations of civil rights to minorities, particularly African Americans. The term derives from the phrase "stay awake."

Sufi – Mystical trend in Islam with metaphysical doctrines, rituals, and institutions. Sufis regard Muhammad as exemplifying the morality of God. They consider Muhammad to be their leader and spiritual guide. See **Muhammad**.

Taiji –Also Romanized as *tai chi*. Short for *taijiquan*, a series of meditative martial-arts exercises that originated in China most likely during the 15th century. They consist of relaxed, slow, circular movements of energy (*qi*) focused on the breath and said to connect the Earth and sky. The practice is rooted in the Neo-Confucian philosophy of the Song Dynasty (960-1279 CE), which intentionally fused Daoist, Buddhist, and Confucian traditions. See *qi*.

Taiyi – Deity in ancient Chinese religion, known as the Great Oneness or the Supreme God of Heaven and associated with the figure of the Yellow Emperor, also known as the Yellow God of the Northern Dipper and as Huangdi. From 2852 to 2070 BCE, northern Chinese people came to worship the Three Sovereigns, said to have been god-kings, and the Five Emperors, classified as sages. These figures are believed to have introduced to humanity fire, home-building, medicine, the calendar, and writing. Huangdi's wife is credited with promulgating silk production. As Huangdi gained prominence as a deity, he was subsumed into the deity Taiyi, the Supreme Unity first described in the "Nine Songs" in the poetry anthology *Chu Ci* (c. 200 BCE). Worship of Taiyi influenced early Daoism, with the name Taiyi ultimately supplanted by the name Dao.

Tantric – Adjective from the noun *tantra* (literally, "weaving"), any of various scriptures rooted in Hinduism and Buddhism. Hindu *tantra* emphasize how balancing feminine and masculine qualities aid one's spiritual growth. Hindu *tantra* are considered secondary scriptures, classified into Smriti and Shakti types. Buddhist *tantra* consist of various Indian and Tibetan texts, which began appearing in India during the Golden Age between 240 to 605 CE. While many early Buddhist texts appeal for worldly things, from the 8th century onward, the tantric texts focus on union with a deity, sacred sounds, and manipulation of the body to achieve awakening/Buddhahood. Tantric texts and practices spread beyond India. Westerners in Asia during the colonial period learned of *tantra*. Numerous forms of Tantrism exist today. Generally, these forms envision correspondence between the inner person and the wider cosmos. Some forms emphasize exchange of energy through particular sexual positions and rituals. Westerners often misunderstand *tantra* to consist of practices, but historically *tantra* actually refers to techniques for interweaving traditions and teachings into a text or practice. See **Buddha** and **Hinduism**.

The Now – A state of attention, awareness and presence when observation of self, others and one's surroundings is more objective and possible. Choice, intention and efforts are available in the Now as is a new kind of seeing and level of awareness. A spiritual Now.

Truth – Truth spelled with a capital *T* refers to universal truth, as opposed to contextual or subjective truth. Plato believed that knowledge gained through the five senses is opinion, and that to achieve actual knowledge one must use philosophical reasoning. Thus, even scientific reasoning through trial and error achieves truth with a small *t*. Another way to understand the difference between "truth" and "Truth" is through linguistic indefiniteness versus definiteness in terms like "nature" versus "Nature" and "now " versus "the Now." The definite proper noun specifies the entity as solitarily unique. See **Plato**.

Vog – Air pollution resulting from volcanic eruption. When a volcano releases sulfur dioxide and other chemicals, they react with oxygen, moisture, and sunlight—producing vog. The word developed from a combination of the words "volcanic," "smog," and "fog."

Werewolf – Mythological figure in European folklore. The concept of a human who could shape-shift into a wolf was recorded by the Roman author Gaius Petronius Arbiter (27-66 CE). The idea of shape-shifting goes back far in human history to the earliest known practices of totemism and shamanism. The ability to transform oneself into a wolf, also called lycanthropy, has been a frequent motif in European folklore. The legend persisted through the Middle Ages. The British lawyer and author Gervase of Tilbury (1150-1228 CE) wrote about the werewolf. As accusations of witchcraft increased, so did accusations of being a werewolf. As late as the 1800s, people were still being put on trial for lycanthropy. In her best-selling 1992 book *Women Who Run with the Wolves*, the American author, Jungian analyst, and scholar Clarissa Pinkola Estés discusses wolf-centered myths, fairy tales, and folk tales to analyze the Wild Woman archetype. The werewolf is said to transform from human to wolf at the time of the full moon. Modern horror literature, film, and fantasy genres have absorbed the werewolf figure.

Whitman, Walt – (May 31, 1918 – March 26, 1892). Renowned American poet, essayist, and journalist. Following the transcendentalist movement in literature, there emerged the humanist movement, which would be followed by the realist movement. As a humanist, Whitman advocated for the value of human beings along with individual and collective freedom, emphasizing rationalist critical thinking and empirical evidence above dogma and superstition. Whitman's major work, his poetry collection *Leaves of Grass*, was first published in 1855. In the book, he conceived of ordinary people as both characters in his poems and his prospective readers. While some say that he neglected spirituality in favor of celebrating the material world, others say that he exalted the spirituality of the material world. Langston Hughes, respected 20th-century author and advocate for the civil rights of African Americans, extolled Whitman's advocacy for freedom: whether urban workers or rural farmers, and regardless of ethnicity, all deserve freedom from serfdom. In recent times, some have criticized Whitman as racist, pointing for example to his celebratory language about white settlers' westward migrations. They say Whitman's America never existed. Nevertheless, other critics assert, Whitman's championing of democracy is a constructive legacy.

Yang – Active male bright energy within the cosmos. See **yin** and **yinyang**.

Yinyang – In Chinese philosophy, the symbol representing the universal principle of harmony. Harmony of duality is a longstanding, ancient principle. Dual energy channels/forces are complementary, interconnected, and interdependent. Just as shadow cannot exist without light, and just as a human foot has no bottom without its top, *yin* and *yang* are inseparable. Examples of twin forces include active-passive, masculine-feminine, and bright- dark, The interaction of *yin* and *yang* creates something new. See **Yang** and **Yin**.

Yemenja – One of the *orisha* in the Yoruba religion. She is the mother of all 14 major *orisha* and of all humanity, with the breaking of her water during childbirth resulting in great floods. Throughout the Trans-Atlantic slave trade, slaves brought religious traditions with them to the Americas. Across Latin America and the Caribbean, mother deities from *indio* and African religions became syncretized with Catholic religious figures. In Cuba, the Yemanja *orisha* joined with the Virgin Mary. Considered a protector, comforting and cleansing sorrow, worshippers appeal to her for fertility in women, as well as in pregnancy, childbirth, child safety, and healing. She is represented by water, from calm stillness to violent turbulence. See **Orisha** and **Yoruba**.

Yin – Passive female dark energy within the cosmos. See **Yang** and **Yinyang**.

Yoga – Originating in ancient India, meditative physical, mental, and spiritual practices intended to expand one's consciousness beyond the individual level with the cosmos. These practices originated around the 6th to 5th centuries BCE. The 6th-century Indian grammarian Panini described two possible roots of the word *yoga*: *yujir yokga* ("to yoke") and *yud samadhau* ("to concentrate"). Subsequent theorists agreed on the second definition. Experts in *yoga* are called *yogi* (for males) and *yogini* (for females). The goal of yoga practice is *moksha* ("liberation"). Hinduism, Buddhism, and Jainism contain yogic practices and texts, and within each tradition there are various schools. During the 11th century, a Persian Islamic scholar visited India and brought back what he learned about *yoga*. Sunni and Shia branches of Islam rejected it, but some Sufis accepted it. In 2008, Malaysia declared *yoga* blasphemous and *haraam*, but the government relented, permitting *yoga* as exercise so long as it excludes the chanting of religious mantras. Islamic clerics in Singapore, Egypt, and Indonesia have issued *fatwa* against *yoga*. There are *yoga* centers in Iran, although opposed by conservative clerics. The Catholic Church and some evangelical Christian groups have issued directives warning against *yoga* and other practices they classify as New Age. Western *yoga* teachers sometimes face accusations of cultural appropriation. They are asked to take time to learn, study, and practice the depth of South Asian *yoga* traditions, as well as to give back by contributing financially to people in developing regions of the world. See **Buddha** and **Hinduism**.

Yoni – Stylized representation of the Sanskrit word for womb, uterus, vagina, vulva, abode, or source. Within two of the main traditions of Hinduism, Shaktism and

Shaivism, *yoni* symbolizes the feminine cosmic energy. The masculine counterpart of *yoni* is *lingam*. There is also a stylized representation of *lingam*. When the two representations connect, their union represents creation, regeneration, and non-duality. According to some Hindu *tantra*, the *yoni* equals life itself. See **Hinduism**.

Yoruba – Ethnic group of southwest and north-central Nigeria, as well as south and central Benin. Jointly, these areas are considered Yorubaland. Today, more than 40 million Yoruba reside in Nigeria, Benin, Togo, and other parts of West Africa. They are one of the largest ethnic groups in Africa. Most Yoruba speak the Yoruba language and, to varying degrees, perpetuate Yorbua traditions. There is also a Yorbua diaspora. Descendants of slaves who were brought to Europe and the Americas have preserved and passed on some aspects of Yoruba culture. Modern Yoruba emigrants have carried their traditions with them to places around the world. See **Orisha**.

About the Author

Kathryn Waddell Takara, PhD, is the author of seven books of poetry, a biography, and a collection of oral histories. In 2010, she was honored with the American Book Award from the Before Columbus Foundation.

The owner and publisher of Pacific Raven Press, LLC, which has published 18 titles, she is a recognized scholar, celebrated intellectual, and performance artist.

Takara's global travels are reflected in her work as footprints, phantasms, and wings to self-development, consciousness, and a call to conscience.

Born and raised in Tuskegee, Alabama, in the Jim Crow era, Takara is a long time resident of Hawai`i. She has organized major conferences on a variety of African American, Black Diaspora, and minority issues, with national and international scholars. Retired, she is an Associate Professor from the University of Hawai`i at Mānoa, where she developed and taught courses in African American and African history, politics, literature, and culture.

Takara earned her PhD in Political Science and an MA in French. An instructor of college-level French for over ten years, she has given poetry readings in Bordeaux, France; Abidjan, Côte d'Ivoire; and Niamey, Niger. In May 2017, she traveled to China for the eighth time to lecture and perform her poetry at Qingdao University and Beijing University of Foreign Studies. She has appeared in television programs and documentary films, and has given frequent interviews to publications and the media.

She was knighted into the Orthodox Order of St. John, Russian Grand Priory, in 2014. The Order, founded in 1036 is committed to community and international service and healing. Members, originally known as "hospitallers," have included dignitaries and philanthropists of all faiths.

Takara seeks a balanced and aware life. She enjoys her family, friends, pets, travel, meditation, *qigong*, and *taiji*, and reading from her voluminous eclectic library. She also spends time gardening, raising orchids, cooking and writing. She delights in the aesthetics of interior design.

www.kathrynwaddelltakara.com

www.pacificravenpress.co/

Notes

Notes

Notes

www.ingramcontent.com/pod-product-compliance
Lightning Source LLC
Chambersburg PA
CBHW050558300426
44112CB00013B/1969